Ask Dr. K. Fisher

about Animals

Written by
Claire Llewellyn

Illustrated by
Kate Sheppard

KINGFISHER
BOSTON

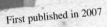

Claire
(the author)

Kate
(the illustrator)

First published in 2007

10 9 8 7 6 5 4 3 2 1
1TR/0307/TECH/SCHOY/157MA/C

Copyright © Kingfisher Publications Plc 2007
Text and concept © Claire Llewellyn 2007

Managing editor: Carron Brown
Coordinating editor: Stephanie Pliakas
Designers: Joanne Brown, Jack Clucas, Tony Cutting, Amy McSimpson
DTP manager: Nicky Studdart
DTP operator: Claire Cessford
Senior production controller: Jessamy Oldfield
Cover designer: Jo Connor

Photograph on p. 10 (top right): Robert Nunnington/Gallo Images/OSF

LIBRARY OF CONGRESS CATALOGING-IN-PUBLICATION DATA
Llewellyn, Claire.
    Ask Dr. K. Fisher about animals / Claire Llewellyn.—1st ed.
    p. cm.
    ISBN-13: 978-0-7534-6043-6
1. Animals—Miscellanea—Juvenile literature. I. Title.
QL49.L778 2007
590—dc22   2006022520

ISBN 978-0-7534-6043-6

Printed in China

KINGFISHER

a Houghton Mifflin Company imprint

222 Berkeley Street

Boston, Massachusetts 02116

www.houghtonmifflinbooks.com

Ask Dr. K. Fisher about . . .

Here's a concerned crocodile mom

Snappy with worry

Dear Dr. K. Fisher,

I'm a Nile crocodile and a responsible parent. My eggs mean everything to me: I guard them, help my young hatch, and then protect them from danger. Some other reptiles I know desert their young. I can't help worrying about the poor little things. Should I call the police?

Uneasy, in the Nile

4

Dr. K. Fisher
Any problem solved!
1 Diving-in-the-Water
Birdsville 54321

Dear **Uneasy,**

There really is no need to worry. Most young reptiles—including lizards, snakes, tortoises, and turtles—do just fine without any parental care. The mother lays the eggs in the ground and leaves them to develop. When the time is right, they hatch by themselves and get on with their lives. It's true—not all of them manage to survive, but many do. You crocodiles make loving moms, but I'm afraid that you're the exception to the reptile rule.

Kind regards,

Dr. K. Fisher

tortoise

turtle

lizard

snake

5

Here's a troubled tadpole

Freaked out!

Dear Dr. K. Fisher,

I thought I was a tadpole, but now I'm not so sure. My body is changing in alarming ways. My head's bulging, my tail's disappearing, and things are beginning to sprout on my body. What is happening to me?

Panic-stricken,
in the pond

tadpole

6

Dr. K. Fisher
Any problem solved!
1 Diving-in-the-Water
Birdsville 54321

Dear **Panic-stricken,**

Don't worry—you are perfectly normal. You're just growing up, and that means you're changing into a frog. Most animals just get bigger as they grow, but you change into something completely new. Those sprouting things will soon be legs for jumping. You'll also get lungs to breathe in air. All of these changes, from an egg to a frog, are part of your wonderful life cycle.

Good luck!

Dr. K. Fisher

egg

tadpole

froglet

frog

Turn the page for **more** about **life** cycles . . .

Dr. K. Fisher's Guide to Life Cycles

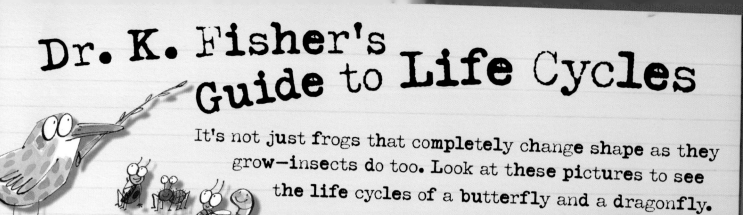

It's not just frogs that completely change shape as they grow—insects do too. Look at these pictures to see the life cycles of a butterfly and a dragonfly.

A butterfly's life

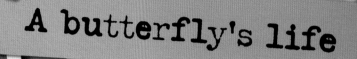

My life began as an egg on a leaf.

I hatched into a caterpillar and ate until my skin split.

My skin molted four more times. Then I changed and became a pupa.

Finally I grew into a beautiful butterfly!

A dragonfly's life

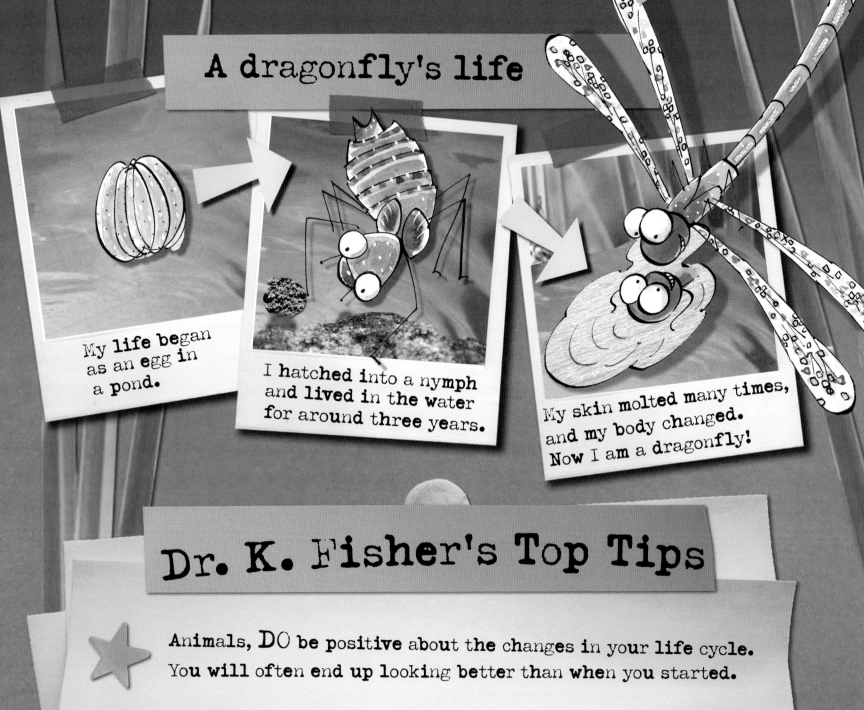

My **life** began as an egg in a pond.

I hatched into a nymph and **lived** in the water for around three years.

My skin molted many times, and **my body changed**. Now I am a dragonfly!

Dr. K. Fisher's Top Tips

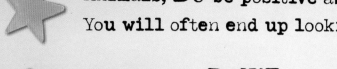

Animals, **DO** be positive about the changes in your **life cycle**. You **will** often end **up** looking better than **when** you started.

Butterflies, **DON'T** move inside your **pupa** too **much**— a predator may spot the slightest twitch.

Dragonfly nymphs, **DO** find a safe place **where** you can molt and **where** predators won't catch you.

How can I build a better nest?

weaverbird (male)

Dear Dr. K. Fisher,

I'm a young male weaverbird, and I can't build a nest. The grasses come loose, the shape is wrong, and the whole thing is a mess. The females are only interested in males who can build. Why is a nest so important to them and how can I make one?

Bumbling Builder, in the bush

weaverbird (female)

10

Dr. K. Fisher
Any problem solved!
1 Diving-in-the-Water
Birdsville 54321

Dear **Bumbling Builder,**

Female weaverbirds get to choose their mates, and the one thing a female wants is a good, strong nest for her eggs. Weaving a nest is complicated work and takes a lot of practice. From the sound of it, this is your first breeding season, and, to be honest, you don't stand much chance against the more experienced males. Try to forget about the females this year. Focus on your nest-building skills instead. I'm sure that next year your luck will change.

Best wishes,
Dr. K. Fisher

adoring females

11

A **tall** story

Dear Dr. K. Fisher,

I'm a giraffe with long legs and a gangly, seven-foot-long neck. I'm so tall that it's embarrassing. All of the other animals stare at me, and it's awkward bending down to their level.

Why am I so tall, and is there anything I can do to be more like the others?

self-conscious, in the **savanna**

zebra

antelope

goat

giraffe

eats from top of tree

Dear **Self-conscious,**

You should be thankful for your neck: it helps you get your meals. There's not a lot to eat in your neck of the woods (excuse the pun)—just a few thorny acacia trees. Other animals chew on the tough branches at the bottom of the trees. But only you, with your long legs and neck, can reach the tender, leafy branches at the top. You are truly a very lucky animal!

Kind regards,

Dr. K. Fisher

eat from bottom of tree

Turn the page for **more** about **feeding** . . .

13

Dr. K. Fisher's Guide to Feeding

All of the animals on these pages have developed very long body parts to help them feed on their favorite foods. It's taken them thousands of years to develop the perfect body parts.

Elephant

Habitat: Grasslands and forests
Diet: Grasses, roots, bark, and fruit
Special body part: Five-foot-long trunk for digging and pulling

Aye-Aye

Habitat: Forests
Diet: Nuts, shoots, and insects
Special body part: Long finger hooks insects out of bark

Flamingo

Habitat: Lakes and lagoons
Diet: Snails, worms, and shrimp
Special body part: Long neck reaches down to lakebed

Toucan

Habitat: Rain forests
Diet: Fruit
Special body part:
Ten-inch-long beak
reaches fruit at the ends
of twigs and branches

Anteater

Habitat: Grasslands
and forests
Diet: Ants and termites
Special body part:
23-inch-long sticky
tongue slurps up insects

Dr. K. Fisher's Top Tips

Finding food takes a lot of effort. DO feed on food that other animals cannot reach. Life will be much easier.

If your chosen food is small in size (like ants) or short in nutrients (like leaves), DO be prepared to gather a lot.

DO make use of any body part you have (tusks, hooves, paws, claws, tentacles, or teeth) in order to find your food.

Here's a mackerel that wants a change

TIME TO LEAVE?

Dear Dr. K. Fisher,

I'm a mackerel, and I'm tired of swimming in a school. Millions of us mackerel swim together. We're all identical to each other, and where the others go, I have to follow. Sometimes I crave a different life—one where I can be myself and do my own thing. Would I be foolish to leave the school and strike out on my own?

Want to be Alone,
in the ocean

mackerel

Dr. K. Fisher
Any problem solved!
1 Diving-in-the-Water
Birdsville 54321

Dear **Want to be Alone,**

Without question, you are safer in a school. The open ocean has few places to hide, and a lone mackerel is an easy target for sharks and other hunters. The school offers you safety in numbers. If a shark approaches, you all bunch up together. If it charges, you dart off in different directions, leaving the shark confused. Unless you want a short life, I must advise you to stay where you are.

Yours sincerely,

Dr. K. Fisher

shark

17

Here's a ladybug with a spotty problem

look at me!

Don't

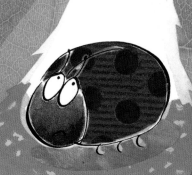

ladybug

Dear Dr. K. Fisher,

I'm a ladybug, and I'm covered in spots. Whatever I do, I can't get rid of them. I try to hide myself away, but there's no way anyone can miss me, because my wing cases are bright red. Please, please send me a cure!

Feeling Awkward,

in the ivy

18

12-spotted ladybug

two-spotted ladybug

14-spotted ladybug

water ladybug

Dr. K. Fisher
Any problem solved!
1 Diving-in-the-Water
Birdsville 54321

Dear **Feeling Awkward,**

The very idea of a ladybug hiding away! Besides being an attractive beetle, you are colorful and spotted for a reason. Most insects hide to avoid being eaten, but you have a better way to survive: you smell and taste very bad! Any bird that tries eating a ladybug spits it out on the spot and never makes the same mistake again, because your bright colors help remind it. Far from being a weakness, your looks are your greatest strength!

Warm regards,

Dr. K. Fisher

pine ladybug

eyed ladybug

nine-spotted ladybug

Turn the page for **more** about **warning colors** . . .

19

Dr. K. Fisher's Guide to Warning Colors

Many animals have stings and sprays to defend themselves when they're under attack. These animals have bright colors or markings that communicate their powerful weapons and warn predators to stay away!

WARNING

poison-arrow frog

Brightly colored skin contains a deadly poison

WARNING

skunk

Black-and-white stripes warn others of its bad-smelling spray

WARNING

coral snake

Red, yellow, and black rings advertise its poisonous bite

WARNING

bee

Yellow-and-black stripes tell the world that it has a painful sting

Dr. K. Fisher's Top Tips

 If you **have** warning colors, DO make sure that **everyone** can see them. It's no **use** hiding yourself away.

 DO **have** confidence in your warning colors, **even if** you are unarmed. Hover flies flaunt their stripes, but they can't sting.

 If a **predator** gets too close in spite of your warning colors, DO hiss, **buzz**, or puff yourself up to scare it away.

21

Here's a lovesick spider in deadly danger

Date or dinner?

Dear Dr. K. Fisher,

I'm a male orb web spider, and I need your help. There's a sweet spider around here, and I'd really like to get to know her better. But I've heard some terrible rumors: do females really kill males after mating? Although I'm crazy about her, I'd like to survive. What do you think I should do?

Lovesick but Wary,
on the Web

orb web spider
(male)

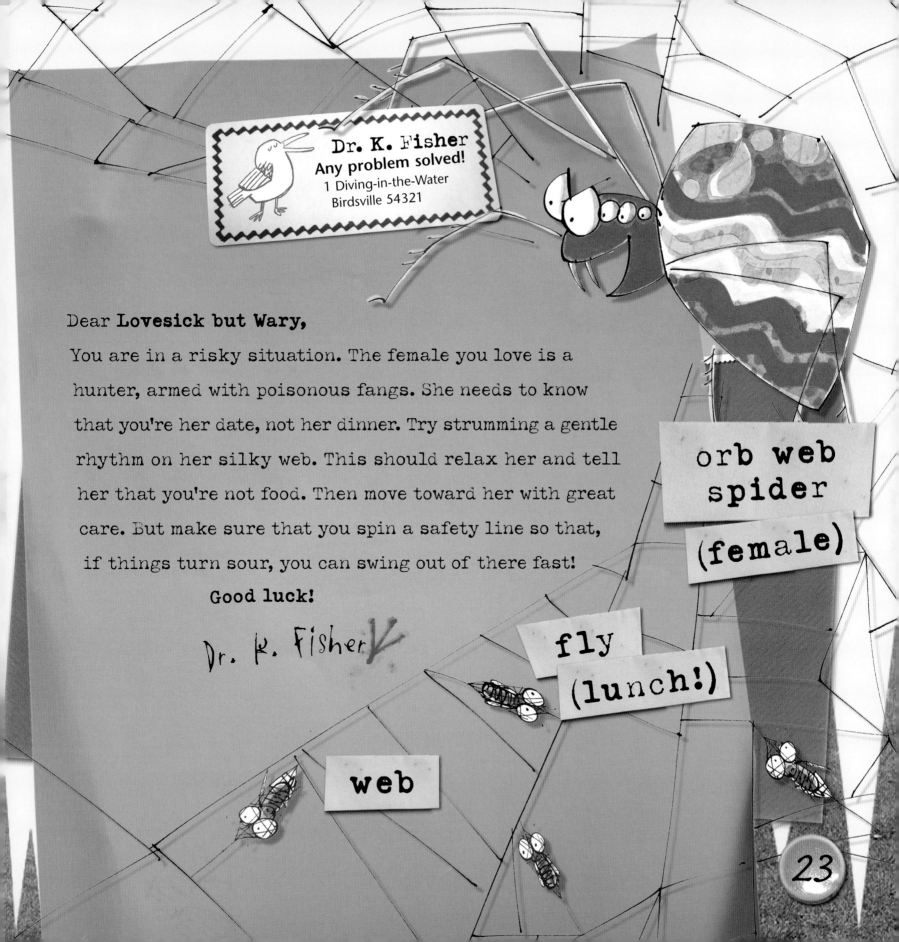

Dear **Lovesick but Wary,**

You are in a risky situation. The female you love is a hunter, armed with poisonous fangs. She needs to know that you're her date, not her dinner. Try strumming a gentle rhythm on her silky web. This should relax her and tell her that you're not food. Then move toward her with great care. But make sure that you spin a safety line so that, if things turn sour, you can swing out of there fast!

Good luck!

Dr. K. Fisher

orb web spider (female)

fly (lunch!)

web

Dr. K. Fisher
Any problem solved!
1 Diving-in-the-Water
Birdsville 54321

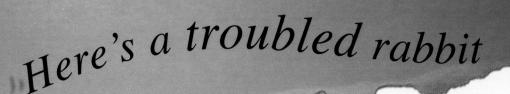

Grass is best

weasel

Dear Dr. K. Fisher,

I'm a rabbit, and I would like to know why so many animals want to eat me. I'm hunted by weasels, owls, foxes, cats, dogs, and ferrets. Why can't everyone just eat grass and try to get along?

Give Peace a Chance, in the meadow

THE MEADOW
SEPT. 2ND
MAIL

Dr. K. Fisher

rabbit

24

Dr. K. Fisher
Any problem solved!
1 Diving-in-the-Water
Birdsville 54321

Dear **Give Peace a Chance,**

The world is not perfect for rabbits, but it isn't perfect for foxes and owls either. These meat eaters (known as carnivores) have to catch every meal. They eat plant eaters (known as herbivores), who, in turn, eat plants. Carnivores, herbivores, and plants—you're all connected in a food chain. I would advise you to count your blessings. Your long ears help you hear trouble coming, and you can run very fast.

With best wishes,

Dr. K. Fisher

fox

Turn the page for **more** about **food chains** . . .

Dr. K. Fisher's Guide to Food Chains

All animals need food because it gives them the energy necessary to **live** and grow. In a food chain, energy is passed from the sun to **plants**, from plants to **herbivores**, and on to the carnivores that feed on them.

An Arctic food chain

I EAT

I EAT

moss
(plant)

caribou
(herbivore)

wolf
(carnivore)

A rain-forest food chain

fruit (plant)

I EAT

I EAT

monkey (herbivore)

eagle (carnivore)

Dr. K. Fisher's Top Tips

 Carnivores, catching food is never easy. DO try to avoid injuries and always keep yourself in tiptop condition.

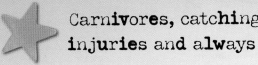 Herbivores, DON'T worry too much about being prey. Many of you have big families, and you always outnumber the hunters.

 Everyone, DO care for plants. They supply us with food to eat, and, without them, we would starve.

27

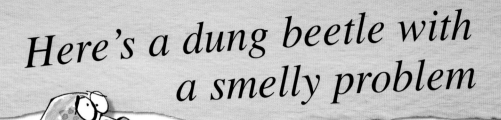

Here's a dung beetle with a smelly problem

Life stinks!

Dear Dr. K. Fisher,

I'm a young dung beetle, and I've made a shocking discovery: all I can eat is dung (poop)! The other dung beetles are obsessed with it and race off to gobble up droppings as they splatter on the ground. Or they roll it into balls, take it home, and lay their eggs in it.

Yuck! Why do I have this disgusting diet?

Outraged, in the manure

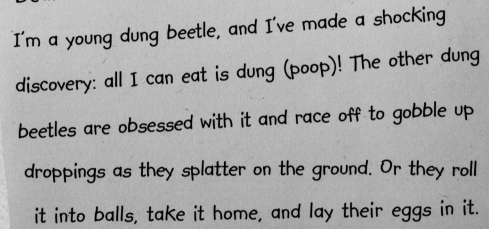

dung beetle

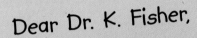

Dr. K. Fisher
Any problem solved!
1 Diving-in-the-Water
Birdsville 54321

Dear **Outraged,**

I sympathize, I really do, but many creatures have a taste for dung. Along with flies, worms, and bacteria, you are one of nature's garbage recyclers, and you do the world a great service. Without you, we would be drowning in dung. By eating it and breaking it down, you recycle the important nutrients that it contains—and make the soil a better place, where plants can live and grow. Be proud of the work that you do!

Yours respectfully,

Dr. K. Fisher

flies

worm

29

Glossary

bacteria
Tiny creatures that live in soil, water, and air.

carnivores
Meat-eating animals.

develop
To grow and change.

diet
The food that an animal naturally eats.

habitat
The natural home of an animal or a plant.

hatch
To break out of an egg.

herbivores
Plant-eating animals.

life cycle
The growing process of an animal or a plant, from the start of its life until it's fully grown.

molt
To shed skin during the growth process so that the body can get bigger.

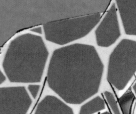

30

nutrients
Substances that can be taken in by an animal or a plant to help it grow.

nymph
The young life stage of an insect, which later changes into an adult without becoming a pupa.

predators
Animals that hunt other animals for food.

prey
Animals that are hunted and eaten by other animals.

pupa
The stage in an insect's life cycle when it changes into an adult.

recycle
To break down something into simple parts, which can then be used again.

reptiles
Cold-blooded animals, such as snakes, that have tough, scaly skin and live on land.

savanna
Dry grassland in east Africa.

Index